MW01047948

A PARADE OF SOVIET HOLIDAYS

A PARADE OF SOVIET HOLIDAYS

BY JANE WERNER WATSON
ILLUSTRATED BY BEN STAHL

GARRARD PUBLISHING COMPANY
CHAMPAIGN, ILLINOIS

Library of Congress Cataloging in Publication Data

Watson, Jane (Werner) 1915–
   A parade of Soviet holidays.

   (Around the world holidays)
   Summary: Discusses the significance of the
most important Russian holidays throughout the
year and the means of celebrating them.

   1. Festivals—Russia—Juvenile literature.
[1. Festivals—Russia. 2. Holidays—Russia]
I. Stahl, Ben F., illus. II. Title.
GT4856.A2W37   394.2'6947   73–12785
ISBN 0–8116–4951–2

CONTENTS

A PARADE OF SOVIET HOLIDAYS

1. A FROSTY NEW YEAR

A Party at the Kremlin

The day is snapping cold. Wintry sunlight glitters on the snowy ground. Lines of parents and children bundled in warm winter clothes are gathering at the doorways of theaters and concert halls. While they wait to enter, they stamp their feet for warmth.

Each child holds a ticket tightly in his mittened hand. This ticket, bought by parents at their office or factory or by the child at school, is the key that will unlock a magic world—the New Year's party.

New Year's Day has largely replaced Christmas as a holiday in the Soviet Union. The Communist government discourages religious observances of all kinds, but Soviet officials did not want to take the joy of holidays out of people's lives. To replace Christmas celebrations, they have started winter festivals in some cities, with special plays and operas and shows of all kinds. As for the Christmas tree and the Old Man of Christmas with his sack full of toys, these have lived on by simply changing their names. They have become the New Year's tree and Grandfather Frost.

New Year's Day is now a children's holiday celebrated in all the fifteen republics of the vast Soviet Union. From desert towns of central Asia to the frozen Arctic, the two weeks' holiday from school, which starts in late December and runs until mid-January, is a lively time for young people. Parties are given in the clubs attached to most collective farms, large plants, and offices. There are parties in city opera houses and concert halls, and in the House of Unions. For children who live in Moscow, though, the biggest party of all is held in the Kremlin, in the handsome modern Palace of Congresses.

The Kremlin is the big old red-walled fortress at the center of Moscow. Inside its walls is a space at least as large as a dozen ordinary city blocks. It holds tall white churches, one-time palaces, living quarters for officials, a great museum, and the huge Palace of Congresses or Soviets.

Most Moscow children have visited the Kremlin on school excursions. During the winter many have coasted down the sloping snowy banks outside the walls on their sleds. But a visit to the Kremlin for a New Year's party is different.

As many as 50,000 children crowd into the Palace of Congresses for one of the series of New Year's parties. They check their heavy coats, caps, and scarves at the cloak room. But they are careful to hold on to their tickets!

Inside, the huge hall has been transformed into a fairyland. An immensely tall pine tree towers almost out of sight. It shimmers and glows and glitters with hundreds of colored lights and ornaments of tinsel and spun glass. Nearby stands genial Grandfather Frost, dressed all in white. He is in charge of the festivities. Little Snowflake, or the Snow Maiden, and her helpers, dressed as beautifully as ballet stars, assist him.

Grandfather Frost takes the place of Saint Nicholas in the hearts of Russian children. When parents buy special New Year's gifts for their boys and girls in department stores, it is often possible to arrange for Grandfather Frost in full costume to deliver the gifts to the children in their homes. Presents are important!

When a child's eyes have become accustomed to all the bright glitter of the party hall, he begins to look for something special. Yes, there it is—a huge box, and beside it a jolly clown. Each child gives the clown his ticket to the party and receives, in return, a brightly wrapped present from the box.

It is fun to shake the parcel a little, to try to guess what is inside. There is sure to be a toy, something for fun, perhaps a book, colored pencils or crayons. And every child receives some sweets—perhaps caramels wrapped in bright paper or a tangerine from the Georgian Republic far to the south.

At the front of the grand hall is a stage. Sometimes operas and ballets and concerts are presented there. Today clowns bounce and tumble and joke with the children. Troops of dancers in bright

costumes leap and prance and kick their heels. Choruses sing to the music of twanging strings.

Older boys and girls, in grades nine and ten in school, dress in their best and go out in the evening to New Year's balls. Some boys go in groups with other boys, grumbling about having to dress up, and making jokes among themselves. Shy girls join groups of girl friends. Other boys and girls go in pairs.

These dancing parties are held in Young Pioneers Palaces, in schools, in clubs or theaters. The theaters in most Soviet cities are spacious, with wide, brightly lighted halls on several levels and grand staircases between. The boys and girls, when they are not dancing, wander from one room to another.

In one hall a singing group may be performing, while in another an orchestra plays classical music. A troop of young actors may offer a play. And on an upper floor of the theater, there is sure to be a buffet —a restaurant with cold dishes, sweets, and soft drinks displayed for sale on a counter. Then at the end of the evening, to step out into the frosty darkness of streets strung with colored lights is the perfect finish to a memorable New Year's ball.

14

Winter Sports

New Year's parties are the high points of the holiday, but the two-week vacation from school is full of fun. Special plays for children are given in the big theater. There is plenty of time for winter sports too.

Children, pulling their small wooden sleds behind them, head for open patches of snow. If they live near a frozen stream, they slide down the high bank onto the ice. If there is no stream or slope close at hand, parents may pile up snow into a mound for the sleds to coast down.

Out on the ice some children knock pieces of wood around with heavy sticks in informal ice hockey games. Others put on thick felt boots and simple wooden skis and go cross-country skiing.

In old Russia, the favorite winter sport was riding in sleighs drawn by troikas, the famous three-horse teams. There are not many troikas to be seen anymore, but out in the country children still enjoy gliding across snowy fields and along ice-clad rivers in horse-drawn sleighs. One doesn't need a troika to have outdoor fun during the winter holiday!

Army Day and Boys' Day—February 22

Down the snowy streets of Soviet cities band music blares. Crowds gather along sidewalks to watch, as red banners fly above marching troops. This is Army Day, honoring the founding of the Soviet army.

As many military men as can be spared have a day's holiday from work. Apart from the parade, it is a day of recreation, and the men will receive small presents from their relatives in honor of the festive day.

In recent years Army Day has taken on an additional meaning. It is also a "Boys' Day." Boys do not have a day free from work. They go to school as usual.

For most boys a small gift starts the day off well. It may be something to wear, or a new book. At school there is more excitement and exchanging of small gifts. Boys receive presents from their close friends and from the girls who share with them the slant-topped double desks of Russian school rooms. Every classroom has a holiday air on this special day for boys.

Women's Day—March 8

The girls' turn comes just a couple of weeks after Boys' Day. On Women's Day the boys bring small gifts for their seatmates or other girls in their class.

Officially, the day is set aside for honoring women who have been outstanding during the past year in some field of activity. A woman may have written a good book or produced the most yards of silk of any weaver, or have been the best worker on her collective farm. She may be an outstanding railway worker, doctor, dancer, or soldier in the armed forces. In the Soviet Union women work in all fields, and it is on Women's Day that they receive their ribbons or medals from the government.

All women are given special attention when Women's Day comes, though. Most of them have jobs outside their homes, and on this day they are excused from their work in offices and factories and on collective farms.

On the day before the holiday, their male co-workers bring them small gifts—perhaps a single flower, a little candy, or a small container of perfume. Often there is a little celebration in the place

17

where the women are employed. The men may give a short play or concert, and they prepare the refreshments for the ladies too.

In the gray early twilight, many men hurrying home from work turn in at the lighted doorways of shops along the streets near their homes. Others stop at sidewalk flower booths. In spite of the late-winter cold, these glassed-in flower booths are busier than usual. Soon the men hurry on, carrying their last-minute gifts for wives, mothers, sisters, or daughters. When they reach home, they may find friends gathering for a festive meal. The men among the guests are sure to bring flowers or perfume or candy for their hostess.

Often a family goes out to a restaurant for a holiday meal. The father calls the restaurant to reserve a table, so that the holiday dinner will be specially pleasant.

Every cluster of new apartment buildings has a restaurant in the shopping center attached to it. Since every restaurant has musicians playing and usually there is space for dancing, everyone has a good time on this pleasant holiday.

18

2. WELCOME TO THE SPRING

Pancake Day

The black iron griddle on the stove top sizzles and sputters with hot fat. Onto the griddle pancake batter is poured in a thick golden stream. The pancakes, as round as the sun and almost as yellow, soon bubble and brown. They are flipped over quickly, then stacked in high piles on plates.

Lots of pancakes are needed, for this is Pancake Day. In the days before the revolution, Pancake Day was Shrove Tuesday, the day before Ash Wednesday at the start of the Lenten season of the Christian church. The week leading up to Ash Wednesday was called Butter Week.

In the church calendar, the forty days of Lent before Easter Sunday are a time for repenting one's sins and doing without things. Most churchgoing Russians used to give up eating fish, meat, eggs, and dairy products for that period. Some still do. So on the days before the long fast, they feast.

People like to eat their fill of pancakes on this day, whether or not they follow the teachings of the church. Big, thin pancakes are wrapped around a filling of preserved fruit—tart cherries are a favorite —and topped with pale smooth sour cream. Small round pancakes called *blinis* are served with mounds of sour cream, fine-chopped hard-boiled eggs, pale green bits of minced onion, and—most important— the delicious small gray fish eggs known as caviar. Everyone heaps his favorite combination on the small pancake base.

The pleasant custom of the pancake feast started far, far back in the past, when the sun was worshiped as a god in Russia, and in other lands as well. Round pancakes, like the sunflowers in the fields, were thought of then as symbols of the friendly power of the sun.

20

Easter

Every spring girls and women in some Soviet lands boil eggs and color them with dyes and paints. The egg, the cradle of life, has been a symbol of rebirth in the festival of spring for uncounted years. The Christian church took over this spring festival to celebrate the resurrection of Christ.

Christianity is no longer a state religion in Russia or in any other republic of the Soviet Union. Few Christian churches—or, for that matter, Moslem mosques or Jewish synagogues—offer services these days. But after a long winter the return of spring and the rebirth of life in nature are reason enough for a celebration. The old ways linger on in people's hearts too. So Easter is still celebrated as a religious holiday by some people. And Easter eggs are colored and Easter breads baked for the holiday season by more.

On the evening of the Saturday before Easter, in Russia and the Ukraine, the whole family used to go to church. Some still do today. The woman of the household wrapped her *kulich*—the tall, round, frosted loaf of Easter bread—in a big clean kerchief and carried the fresh bread to church to be blessed.

21

Other members of the family took along some decorated eggs or perhaps the meat pies called *pirok*, made with light, risen dough and seasoned with cinnamon. They wanted these foods to be blessed too. And everyone carried a candle.

When they arrived, the church was aglow inside with golden lamplight. The light was reflected softly from the rows of paintings, called *icons*, of saints on the screen at the front.

In the days before the revolution, everyone attended the Easter services. Rich and poor, masters and servants, government officials, students, businessmen, workers and their families all stood side by side.

When the priests intoned the Lord's Prayer, or when the Song of the Cherubim rose through the candle-scented air, everyone sank to his knees on the hard floor.

At last the priest cried out, "Christ is risen!" Then from the candles on the altar the light was passed from hand to hand. Soon every candle in the church glowed with its own small golden flame. Every heart felt uplifted as the worshipers answered, "He is risen indeed!"

As the priest moved out of the church, the congregation followed, all singing and carrying their lighted candles. Swinging his censer to spread its fragrant smoke, the priest circled the churchyard with his assistants. There he blessed the Easter bread of the people who had not been able to find room inside the church. All around the dark yard the long procession of small lights bobbed against the blackness of the spring night.

Usually there is a hint of softness in the air by Easter. So when the procession left the churchyard, no one was in a hurry to go home. With candles still alight in their left hands, people strolled down the streets.

Whenever they met anyone, they paused. "Christ is risen," they said in greeting.

"He is risen indeed," came the reply.

Then rich or poor, stranger or friend, everyone was greeted with a right-handed hug and the three kisses that symbolize the Trinity—God the Father, Son, and Holy Spirit.

At home each family found the table set for a festive meal. This midnight feast was a special celebra-

24

tion, because for the forty days of Lent preceding Easter, really devout families had eaten mainly cereals, potatoes, vegetable oils, and pickles. They had taken not so much as one bite of any food that came from living creatures.

It was a real treat to find on the table tender young lamb, golden-skinned chicken, perhaps a crisp-crusted suckling pig. Of course there were kulich, the Easter bread, and the special Easter cake as well.

This cake, called *pashka*, the word for Easter, was made of cottage cheese with dried fruit and nuts. The mixture was pressed into a wooden mold, usually in the form of a steep-sided pyramid. When the cake was removed from its mold, it was decorated with candy eggs or brightly colored real eggs.

On Easter Sunday in towns and cities, the men went visiting. The women and children stayed at home to receive the callers and see that they were well fed. In each home the table was spread with the best cloth, which was covered with platters of bread, greens, and cold meats—chicken, goose, duck, and lamb. There were also bottles of vodka and various other things to drink.

25

Easter Monday was a holiday for schoolchildren and for most workers to rest up from these festivities.

In the Baltic republics Easter was somewhat different, because the churches were Protestant rather than Eastern Orthodox. Services were held on Easter Sunday morning rather than at midnight the night before. And after the church service, families paid calls on their friends.

Easter eggs had an important place in the celebration in these northern lands too. The eggs were boiled, some with onion skins in the water, some with young birch leaves. Others had ferns fresh from the damp spring woods tied around the shells in a layer of cheese cloth.

The ferns gave the eggshell a warm grayish tone, the birch leaves pale green. But the onion skin colored the eggshell a glowing orange yellow, and this color of the sun was the favorite. Colored inks were used to decorate the tinted eggs with drawings of flowers, patterns of lines, or other designs.

The prettiest eggs were put aside to be given as gifts. Some of the rest the children tucked into their pockets. After the church service two youngsters would each pull out an egg and knock the two sharply against each other. The one whose egg did not crack won the cracked egg—or another in its place. Some lucky players assembled whole pocketfuls of eggs.

Another game, the egg roll, called for a small wooden chute. The chute was about a foot high, with low rails guarding a slide wide enough for an egg to roll down easily. One egg was placed out in front of the slide at some distance. The players took turns, each rolling one egg at a turn down the slide. If an egg failed to touch one of those out in front, it stayed where it landed. A successful player got his own egg back and also the one his had clicked against.

Meanwhile grown-ups hung very long ropes from tall trees for swings. Teen-age girls and boys and also young adults in pairs rode in these swings, pumping with bent knees. Higher and higher they went until their wide arcs took them up into the tree branches. Occasionally, with a stomach-twisting thrill, they looped up and over the branch. This was considered too scary for the younger children, but it was certainly a lively way to welcome the northern spring.

Children's Book Holiday

April brings a ten-day spring vacation from school. Special posters appear on walls and fences. They announce plays for children, young people's concerts, and exhibitions of children's books.

Busloads of village children come into the cities for special performances at the theaters. Many of them also have time to wander about the big halls given over to the exhibitions of books.

Children's Book Holiday is a special spring treat. Book shops fill their windows with the newest brightly illustrated books for young readers. Youngsters write letters to their newspaper, *Pioneer Truth*, about their favorite books. During the Book Holiday they may get a chance to meet the authors and illustrators of these favorites. For many people who work on children's books appear at the exhibition halls to tell the young readers about their work.

Subbotnik, Lenin's Birthday

It is a Saturday in April. All over Russia parks are bustling with unusually large work crews. Men and women hoe, trim bushes, pull weeds, and set out neat rows of flowering plants in beds of black soil. Some of the workers handle their tools rather clumsily, but they all seem in the best of spirits.

At hospitals, crews wash windows and scrub floors and do other tasks. Now and then they straighten up and stretch to rest muscles that are not used to this kind of work.

Still other groups of workers who do not seem quite at ease with their tools appear around town. They are busy cleaning public buildings, streets, and riverbanks. All these people are giving one day's work— at some unfamiliar task—in honor of the birthday of V. I. Lenin, the first premier of the Soviet Union.

Lenin was born on April 22, 1870, as Vladimir Ilyich Ulyanov. "Lenin" was the name he took when he joined a group that worked toward a revolution in Russia. It was under his forceful leadership that the Russian Revolution succeeded in taking over the government in 1917. Because Lenin was determined that working people should rise up and rule the country, his birthday is celebrated with *subbotnik*, a day of work, on the Saturday closest to April 22.

On the birthday itself, plays and movies and television programs present scenes from Lenin's life. In many clubs and schools there are also lectures, discussions, and special programs.

Every Russian schoolchild is well acquainted with Lenin. For those whose homes are in or near Moscow, very likely their first school excursion is a visit to the red stone tomb of Lenin just outside the walls of the Kremlin on Red Square. Even before he starts school, though, a Russian child will have seen his parents leave home early on an April Saturday to work at some subbotnik task in honor of "Papa Lenin."

Cosmonauts' Day—April 12

It was on April 12, 1961, that Major Yuri Gagarin was launched into orbit from a base in Siberia. He circled the earth once in a spacecraft called *Vostok I* —the first human being to travel in space—and landed safely.

There have been other Russian space travelers in the years since 1961. Russia, which fifty years ago was a backward agricultural country, takes great pride in its technical achievement. Space exploration is a source of special pride. So it is not surprising that the government decided to establish a new holiday to honor all the brave cosmonauts. Instead of a parade down city streets, though, this holiday features a grand display of aircraft moving in formation across the sky.

Cosmonauts' Day is not the only occasion for an air show. An even bigger one comes in August, on Aviation Day. Then thousands from Moscow travel out to the Sports Airport for a spectacular show. All types of Soviet aircraft, both civilian and military, are part of the performance. The newest supersonic jets streak overhead, leaving long white vapor trails against the brilliant blue sky. There are gliders and sailplanes as well as powered craft.

Beneath some of the planes, masses of white parachutes burst into bloom as airborne troops float toward earth. After a moment of hushed silence, the crowd roars its approval.

When night falls, the celebration is climaxed, as are many Soviet holidays, with a brilliant display of fireworks splashing patterns of colored stars against the dark sky.

May Day—May 1, 2

Offices, factories, and schools are all closed for the May Day holiday. This is an international Labor Day, but it has special importance in the Soviet Union where everyone is considered to be a worker. For most families it is a busy day that starts even earlier than usual.

Some fathers and grandfathers volunteer to march in the May Day parade to represent their factories. They may take small boys and girls of the family with them to march with the group.

Some of the young people hurry off to meet friends from their school class. Particularly if this is their last year in school, they like to march together. Other members of the family make their way together to the central square of the city to see the big parade.

Every Soviet city has a parade, but the most famous is naturally the one in Moscow, the capital of the Soviet Union. This parade centers on Red Square, the heart of so many celebrations.

All the metro lines—the deep subways reached by steep flights of moving stairs—are crowded with family groups on the morning of May Day. When the

34

family comes up the stairs to the open air, they may have to take a moment to get their bearings. Though they know they are very near Red Square, it is hard to recognize even familiar streets this morning. It is scarcely possible even to see the square through the crowd!

As the grown-ups try to look over the heads of the people, they find the air above dancing with colored balloons. Red, blue, orange, green—the bright balls glitter in the sunlight. They bob among red streamers and huge red banners, several stories high, strung between buildings and along flat walls.

The streets leading into Red Square from all sides are blocked off with barricades manned by policemen. They keep out not only automobiles, trucks and buses, but people on foot as well. For the square must be kept clear for the parade.

Every inch of the pavement behind the barricades is jammed with people. The most desired places are those that face Lenin's tomb, just outside the long red wall of the Kremlin. The tomb is a simple building, broad and low, made of polished dark red stone. It is flanked on either side with temporary reviewing

stands. But the highest officials of the government will review the parade from the flat roof of the tomb itself.

Long before the officials climb the hidden stairs to take their places, some of the grown-ups are wondering just who will be seated there. One way to tell who is becoming more powerful in the government —or less important—is to see who has a place in the main reviewing stand for the May Day parade.

A few blocks away, across the Moscow River, marchers find their places in line. They approach the square by way of a bridge, marching in ranks twenty persons wide. Each group has a banner to carry. The banner or flag may tell what a certain factory has accomplished, or which school's students are marching. It may have some popular slogan or a portrait. Paraders in old Russia used to carry portraits of the tsar and pictures of Christian saints. Now instead they honor men who fought in the revolution or in more recent wars.

Proudly the broad ranks pass the reviewing stand. Their lines stretch off into the distance as far as the eye can see. Now and then there is a pause while some group—most likely a marching band—paces out a special formation in the heart of the square. Perhaps the marchers spell out the initials of the Communist party. Everyone marches with great spirit —factory workers, members of the Young Communist organization called the Komsomol, and the Young Pioneers.

The 300 Young Pioneers, boys and girls between ten and fourteen years of age, are easy to spot in their white shirts and red scarves. Each of the twenty-nine districts of Moscow takes its turn at selecting boys and girls from its area who will march in a given year's parade.

May Day can be cold in Moscow. One year snow fell. Each of the Young Pioneers who marched that year was given an award from the government for heroism. The award was a special wrist watch. You may be sure that these have been treasured!

After the parade has passed, the crowd seems reluctant to leave. Many of the children try to push their way toward one of the folding souvenir stands that have been set up. Balloons, stuffed toy animals, and assortments of the popular lapel pins attract

38

them. But the holiday is by no means over, so the family does not have much time to spare for the youngsters' shopping.

Every family plans an especially good dinner for May Day and some small gifts for the children. In addition, there are parties in the clubhouses attached to factories, plants, and other places of work.

In the club rooms both parents and children find friends to visit with. They listen to some speeches and then watch a lively variety show of the kind Russians like so much. The factory chorus sings. Some soloists perform and receive bouquets of flowers from families and friends. A theatrical group may present a play or skit. It seems that every Russian has some talent, and most of them enjoy having a chance to perform.

After the show, tables are heaped with good food and drink. Later on an orchestra plays for dancing. Boys and girls are usually yawning long before the holiday celebration ends. But to brighten their sleepy homeward way, fireworks splash against the dark sky with bursts of many-colored flowers and flashing, sailing stars.

The Anniversary of Victory—May 9

World War II is known in the Soviet Union as the Great Patriotic War. Some of the harshest campaigns of that war were fought on Russian soil after the Nazi German army invaded the Soviet Union in June 1941. Many Soviet cities were tumbled into ruins, many millions of people killed. But citizens and soldiers alike fought fiercely to save their homeland. This is why May 9, the Anniversary of Victory at the end of that war, is now a national holiday.

Almost every Soviet city has a huge war memorial set in a green park. Some, like the one in Novosibirsk, list tens of thousands of names of residents of the city who were killed during the war years. Many older people recall the horror of nights of bombing, months of hunger, and years of shortages caused by that war. They still think often of relatives and dear ones they lost.

On the Anniversary of Victory, crowds gather at the war memorials. During the ceremony honoring the war dead, large standing wreaths and smaller bouquets of flowers are placed respectfully around the monument.

40

It is not only on the anniversary that people remember those who died in the war. In some cities it is a custom for brides to take their flowers after the wedding to the war memorial and leave them there as a kind of thank offering.

Young Pioneers' Holiday—May 19

On the cobblestone pavement of Red Square in Moscow, a group of boys and girls line up to form three sides of an open-ended square. One by one the neat, scrubbed ten-year-olds, looking excited and a little scared, step inside the square.

There, each youngster repeats the promises of the Young Pioneers—to be good friends and good citizens. A slightly older friend steps forward and loops the red scarf of the Young Pioneers around the initiate's neck. Then the new member steps proudly back to his place in the formation.

Not all Young Pioneers are initiated on Red Square. That is a special treat for a few. Most of the ceremonies take place in the Young Pioneers' room of the neighborhood school or in the Young Pioneers Palace to be found in any Soviet city.

Becoming a Young Pioneer is a big event in the life of almost every ten-year-old in the Soviet Union. Most children have belonged to the Oktobriades since they were eight years old. (This organization is named for the October Revolution that paved the way for Soviet rule in Russia.) But it is still exciting to become a Young Pioneer.

The Young Pioneers Palace soon becomes a sort of "home away from home" for after-school club meetings, games, and hobby groups of all sorts. Young Pioneers Camps, where boys and girls spend their summer holidays, are located all over the Soviet Union—some deep in the woods, beside a rushing river, others at the seashore. Youngsters make good friends and have fine times at these camps, as well as in the all-year-round clubrooms. It is no wonder then that ten-year-olds are eager to join the Young Pioneers!

Initiations are held three times a year. Most children join at the one that comes soonest after their tenth birthday. One of these three dates is May 19, the anniversary of the founding of the Young Pioneers by Lenin himself.

The Young Pioneers' anniversary is an exciting holiday for boys and girls. There are special theater programs and parades in every city of the Soviet Union, but as usual the biggest celebration is in Moscow.

On special anniversaries of the founding, such as the fifteenth, twenty-fifth, or fortieth—or, in 1972, the fiftieth—outstanding members from all the fifteen republics of the Soviet Union are chosen to travel to Moscow for the event.

This is a great honor, and the visit is an exciting adventure. Those who live fairly near the capital make the trip in buses, perhaps with banners on the sides to tell passersby who they are. From farther away, boys and girls and their leaders may come in big gleaming trains painted dark red or dark green. Or they may go by bus to an airport and board an airliner for an exciting flight.

In Moscow, another bus takes the travelers to a hotel. It may be the huge, shiny-white Russia, with its tall lobbies, hallways longer than a city block, and elevators in which you push the buttons yourself for floor stops.

Sharing a room and bath in a hotel with a friend makes the travelers feel very grown-up. On some of the floors of the hotel, there are rooms called buffets with tables and chairs and counters where one can buy pastries and soft drinks and other snacks. Meals are served in the huge dining room, at long tables so friends can sit together.

At nearby tables are other groups of boys and girls. Often it is possible to guess where they are from by their dress, for most of these groups wear their national dress when they come to Moscow. The boys in long striped and belted robes and small embroidered caps are from central Asia, perhaps. The girls in embroidered aprons and blouses? They could be from the Baltic republics or perhaps Moldavia. Those other girls with black braids and long swirling skirts are surely from the Caucasus in the south, and so are the boys with big fur hats. What about the boys whose baggy pants are tucked into high boot tops? The guessing goes on.

Soon the groups are mingling in the lobby or in front of the hotel. Then hands begin to clap and feet to tap. One or two of the boys and girls step into the

center of the circle and begin to dance, while the rest keep time. Then one of the leaders starts a song. What fun!

On the morning of May 19, all the Young Pioneers march in double lines to the area where the parade forms. It will probably be led by teams of older boys or young men. These are members of the young Komsomols, who are from fifteen to twenty-eight years of age. Some of them carry big red flags that make bright splashes of proud color against the blue sky.

Behind them come the ranks of boys and girls. Some wear their customary short skirts or trousers and the familiar white shirts and red scarves. Others wear their national dress. Still others are dressed in the uniform of a special occupation. They may carry models of rockets, ships, locomotives, or other "tools of a trade."

Some groups carry flags. Others hold the edges of wide banners, or wave tall branches of artificial fruit blossoms. This is such a lively and colorful parade, it is not surprising that high officials are glad to take the time to review it.

3. MAKING THE MOST OF SUMMER

School Is Out!—Late May

It is the last week of May, and all over the Soviet Union school is out. Schools in all the fifteen republics teach the same courses, keep to the same schedule, and close on the same day.

On the last day of classes, all the young people who have finished their final year of secondary school—the tenth year—head for the parks to celebrate.

Clusters of girls carrying handfuls of flowers and groups of boys feeling stiff in their best suits wander across open plazas and down shady paths. They soar through the air on Ferris wheels and other rides. Or they gather around one of their number who has a

48

guitar to strum, and they sing their favorite songs. As the day wears into evening, many groups picnic around bonfires. They sing by flickering firelight, now and then leaping up to dance.

There is still work ahead of these young people. The following week they return to school for final examinations. On the morning of the last day of examinations, they make a quick stop at street flower stands on their way to school. Many buy small bunches of flowers—a few roses or tall white lilies—to take to their teachers.

Graduation Day does not come until late June. Then the boys and girls and their families gather in the auditorium of the neighborhood school for the graduation ceremony. In a typical Moscow school, there will be about seventy-five graduates, most of whom have attended together for all their ten school years.

The evening after they have received their certificates, the boys in dark suits and the girls in white dresses go to a graduation ball. Like the New Year's balls, this may be held in the spacious local opera house or some other public building of the city.

After the ball, the graduates stroll about the town. In Moscow, Red Square is the popular place to gather. Usually groups from various schools stay more or less together. Everyone wants to be with old friends on this night of nights.

Midsummer's Eve—June 21–25

A band of young people, dressed in their best and singing merrily, stroll down a country road near the Baltic Sea. The road is lined with white-barked birch trees. The fragrant scent of fresh-cut hay fills the air.

The hour is late, but the sky still shimmers with pale light, for this is St. John's Day, when, here in the far north, the sky scarcely darkens between very late sunset and very early dawn. This has always been a favorite time to celebrate in northern lands where summer is followed by long winter nights.

All across the gently rolling countryside, from the top of each low hill a light blazes. Barrels filled with wood and tar have been hoisted to the tops of high poles and set afire. These bright, smoky flares glow orange against the pale sky.

Below, in every farmyard a tall bonfire crackles

and blazes a welcome. Some of the old folks say the fires keep witches away.

The young people, still singing their folk songs, gather around the bonfire in one dooryard after another. Seated in a circle on the grass, they drink homemade beer fresh from a wooden keg and eat thick, round slices of homemade caraway cheese. An occasional home may offer bread with the cheese, but new beer and round caraway cheeses are the traditional foods for Midsummer's Eve.

There is a lot of joking and chatter and singing of songs. Some of the young people jump up and start to rollick through the figures of an old folk dance. Others, two by two, drift off into the birch groves "to look for fern blossoms."

There are age-old tales of magic ferns that blossomed at midnight on Midsummer's Eve. Those blossoms could lead to hidden treasure or win you the one you loved. People do not take these old tales very seriously anymore. But still young people wander off into the woods in search of magic blossoms. It is understood by all that the search may take a long time.

Holidays of Nations and Regions

The Soviet Union is made up of fifteen republics, most of which have been nations in their own right at some time in their history. Within these republics a number of areas have been set aside as Autonomous Soviet Socialist Republics. These are areas where large groups of people of a distinctive racial background wish to maintain some of their old ways.

At least a hundred different peoples are joined in the Soviet Union. They speak many different languages, and even write their languages in scripts made up of completely different letters. But all of them are united by a knowledge of the Russian language. And all of them celebrate the Soviet national holidays.

In addition, every region and people have holidays of their own, based on their own past. The Baltic republics—Lithuania, Estonia, and Latvia—share many of their customs and holidays with the Scandinavian countries across the Gulf of Finland and the Baltic Sea. The Karelian Autonomous Soviet Socialist Republic was a part of Finland until World War II, and naturally its people still love familiar

Finnish holidays such as Midsummer's Eve and Christmas.

The Buryats, who have an autonomous republic just north of Outer Mongolia, share many of their customs with the Mongolians. Their traditional religion was a form of Buddhism.

Groups of Jews can be found in many regions and republics. In some areas many of them still attend synagogues and celebrate the old holidays of their religion. These include the Jewish New Year, the Day of Atonement with its twenty-four-hour fast, the Passover with its special feast called the Seder, and Hanukkah, the winter festival of lights.

In the central Asian lands—now the Turkmen, Uzbek, Tajik, and Kirghiz Soviet Socialist Republics —most of the people used to be Moslems. At least one Moslem holiday lives on there. *Bairam*, the final day of the Ramadan fast, is celebrated by many who no longer follow the religion from which it came. It is the national holiday of Uzbekistan.

Some regional holidays are patriotic. The Azerbaidzhan Republic, tucked into the beautiful Caucasus Mountains between the Black and Caspian seas, celebrates on April 28. "This is the date," an Azer-baidzhanian explains, "on which in the year 1920 our republic was established."

The neighboring Georgians, on the other hand, celebrate St. George's Day, February 25, as their national day. St. George is generally pictured on horseback, slaying a dragon. It is for him that the Georgian Republic, for many years a proudly inde-pendent nation, was named.

Many Georgian families give parties in their homes on this day. There is also a festival at the cathedral of Mtskheta, the old capital of the country and still its active religious center.

Busloads of Georgians crowd the town, beside the River Kura, at festival time. The cathedral is easy to find, for it is still largely surrounded by the high protective wall, with watchtowers, that made it a kind of fortress in early days. Of course there are souvenir stands near the cathedral's main gate to supply the festival crowd with mementoes of the holiday. But the sound of music soon draws them into the church.

There, the lofty stone walls shimmer with the soft

jewel tones of 800-year-old paintings of saints and holy scenes. Down the center aisle a solemn processional makes its slow way toward the great golden cross before the altar. Priests and choir chant in harmony, and swinging censers release their smoky fragrance. To the worshipers bowing their heads over folded hands, the Christian religion is very much alive in Georgia.

Armenia is the third of the republics of the Caucasus. It maintains its own special form of the Christian church and celebrates its own saints' days.

Villagers bring small bouquets of flowers to place on the altar of the church dedicated to the saint whose special day it is. Then they stand quietly in the church for some time, watching the priests in their long colored robes conducting the old familiar services. Afterward they visit with friends in the churchyard.

Many regional holidays are not religious but seasonal. In most parts of the Soviet Union when the crops are in, farm folk still take time off for a lively festival, as they have always done in the Russian countryside. Then the heaviest work of the farm year

is over. It is time to celebrate, with plenty to eat and drink, and with races and competitions.

Farmers may compete at plowing straight, deep furrows or at milking cows. Troops of young people compete at dancing and singing. Especially in central Asia, horsemen race for prizes.

Every sport, trade, and pastime, it seems, has its special holiday—and competition—somewhere in the USSR. We shall be able to glimpse only a few of them.

The Tatar Festival of the Plow—June 25

From the top of a tall pole set up in an open field comes the crowing of an angry cock. A cage has been fastened to the top of the pole, and in it a fiery red rooster flaps his wings, shakes his wattle, and crows his rage.

At the foot of the pole, which has been well greased, young men wait their turns to try to bring down the cock. Laughing and joking, they rub their palms on their shirts to dry them. The first one chosen leaps at the pole. Clasping his legs around the smooth wood, he starts to climb. Up he goes for some feet, to the shouts and encouragement of the crowd. But the pole is slippery. He struggles to get a grip above his head, but his hands slide down. Even his strong legs cannot hold him in place. At last he gives up and slips back to the ground. Another young man steps forward to try his luck.

These young men are celebrating the Festival of the Plow, called *Saban Tuy* in their Tatar tongue. The Tatars, or Mongols, of central Asia came to Russia as conquerors in the thirteenth century and ruled for 250 years. The city of Kazan on the Volga River, where this festival is taking place, was the capital of one of the Tatar states. Today many Tatars still live in and around Kazan, and the region has been made a Tatar Autonomous Soviet Socialist Republic. The language and many of the old Tatar customs live on there.

For centuries the Tatars had celebrated the completion of their spring farm work with a festival. This Festival of the Plow is now held on June 25, the day when the Tatar Republic was established. So it is truly a national festival.

After the pole climbing, the audience moves on to

another part of the festival grounds where shiny new earthenware crocks have been spread out on the grass.

The first player here is blindfolded, given a strong stick, and twirled about until he is dizzy. When he is let go, he flails about with his stick, trying to smash one of the crocks.

"Ho there, turn around! You will go into the river before you reach a crock! Do you think they are hung from trees? Very close now! Hit harder the next time!"

The jokes and hints and misdirections shouted from all sides confuse the blindfolded player more than they help him. But at last his toe nudges one of the crocks. He smashes down with his stick. There is a crunching of shattered crockery.

The player rips off his blindfold to see what he has won, for there is a prize hidden in every crock. It may be a shirt, a pair of socks, or even a small radio or electric shaver—protected by a sturdy box.

Wrestling matches and other games come next. But the high point of the festival is horse racing. Tatars still recall the old days when their ancestors were more at home in the saddle than standing on the ground. They still love horses—riding and racing.

A favorite race is the one in which the riders are blindfolded. Handkerchiefs are wrapped around their heads "to keep the wind out" as they tear across the plain, bent low in their saddles. Many a Tatar boy, watching from the sidelines, dreams of the old days when his people raced on horseback across half the world, conquering everything in their path.

Ysyakh, a Yakutsk Holiday

In the far northern basin of Siberia's Lena River lies the Yakutsk Autonomous Soviet Socialist Republic. Yakutia, like the Tatar Autonomous Republic, is entirely surrounded by territory of the huge Russian Soviet Federated Socialist Republic. But it, too, enjoys some local self-government and preserves some of the old ways of its people.

The tribal peoples of Yakutia are related both to the hard-riding Turks of central Asia and to the Eskimo. They used to herd reindeer, fish, and hunt or trap forest animals for their rich pelts. Some still hunt, trap, fish, or raise livestock. But many have

moved into the new towns and cities of this arctic region. They have been to school and now work in factories or build dams, apartments, and river barges. After the barges are built, it is Yakuts who make up the crews that keep the broad Lena River busy with traffic.

These are tough, hardy folk who do not mind winter temperatures of 50 degrees and more below zero. They like lively entertainment, and on their national festival day a great crowd gathers on a grassy field near Yakutsk, the capital city. They are celebrating the brief bright season of the midnight sun. But since it is a national holiday, the day starts with some government officials giving their annual reports and presenting awards to workers. People listen politely, perhaps feeling a bit restless. They are more interested in what follows.

Soon the tables, which have been set up, are loaded with food. These are not dainty refreshments. There is plenty of good boiled beef. Each diner spears big chunks of the beef on long wooden skewers and chews off mouthfuls of the meat. He washes it down with fermented mare's milk—a sort of sour buttermilk—

called *kumiss*, which he drinks from a big carved wooden mug. Bottles of other things to drink appear on the long tables, but kumiss is the true drink of the Yakut people.

When everyone has had enough to eat and drink, the fun begins. Men and boys run foot races, and everyone joins in the dancing. For one dance, called the Hitching Post, a horse is tethered to a post in the middle of an open space. The dancers, young men and women, form a circle around the horse. As they move about the circle in dancing steps, they sing. Often they make up their own words to tell of their joy at having good health, good friends—at just being alive!

"What does the horse tethered out in the center have to do with the dance?" a visitor asks.

Some of the men rub their chins and frown thoughtfully, but no one can give a real answer. The custom is so old that its meaning has been lost in the mists of tribal traditions.

There is no hurry about finishing up the dancing. At midnight the sky is still pale and glowing. It is then that the men line up on their mounts for the horse races. In winter they race dog and reindeer sledges, but they like horses too. So the crowd has a fine time racing and betting on the races, eating, drinking, and dancing, far into the arctic night.

Sports Day in Central Asia

The middle of the big open field is a blur of striped robes and gleaming horses. A cluster of riders surges now this way, now that. The men are *djigits*, the skilled riders for whom the republics of central Asia—Uzbekistan, Kirghizstan, and Tajikstan—are famous. They are playing a rough game called *kopkorg* or *ulak* to celebrate Sports Day, called *Kop Karim* in the Uzbek language.

Before the game, a goat is beheaded with one swift stroke of a sword. The body of the goat is dropped in the middle of the playing field, while the two teams of horsemen line up at either end of the field. To start the game, one rider from each team races down the field toward the carcass. Both men lean down from their saddles, and one manages to snatch up the carcass.

At this signal, both teams charge forward to join

in the game. Everyone hopes to race with the goat to his home boundary. This will mean a victory for his team. It is easier said than done, though. The carcass is pulled and hauled this way and that. Often there is not much left of it by the time some rider gets it back to his home base.

The riders bring to this game the high spirits, riding skill, and determination that made their ancestors fierce and powerful fighters. They have had plenty of practice too. Between the formal games on big Sports Days, village teams battle among themselves. In these games, the carcass is dragged between neighboring villages.

In another strenuous game, two skilled horsemen ride their highly trained mounts out into the center of the field. They shake hands in sportsmanlike fashion. Then they proceed to try to kick each other out of the saddle! This is *Ogdarysh*, wrestling on horseback. Horse and rider must work together as a unit to be successful at this rough sport.

A somewhat milder game is *Kuz kumai* or "Catch the Girl." This is really a race between a girl rider and a young man. The course is 200 yards, but the

girl gets a head start and has the faster horse. She is a skillful rider too, you may be sure. Her legs in dark trousers under a short skirt have a firm grip on the horse's belly. Long black braids stream out behind her from under a small embroidered cap.

The young man bends low in his saddle to try to catch her. If he succeeds, he wins not only applause but a kiss. If he does not, he gets a slash of her whip as they ride back to the starting point and has to face the jokes of his friends.

Bairam, a Moslem Holiday

The courtyard of the old mosque, surrounded by pale brick walls decorated with blue, green, and white patterned tiles, is very large. At one side a group of men stand, chatting quietly. Most of them have white beards and wear the pale blue robes, belted at the waist, which were worn in the old days in central Asia.

The men have gathered for a special service. It is in celebration of Bairam, the holiday at the end of the month of Ramadan in the Moslem religious calendar. Devout Moslems fast from dawn to dark every day during the month of Ramadan and celebrate for three days when it is ended.

Since the Soviet state does not encourage religions, there are not many devout Moslems to be found these days in the central Asian republics. Only a few mosques are still open for services on Fridays, the Moslem Sabbath, and most of the finest old mosques are now museums.

Old customs live on, however, and in Uzbekistan Bairam is still the national holiday. Schools and offices close, but only for one day now instead of three. Many families, even if they do not all attend services at the mosque, may gather to picnic in a nearby grassy park. Perhaps some of the men go to the service. And every family is sure to have a holiday feast.

In the old days, when most Uzbeki families raised sheep and goats, a lamb or kid was slaughtered for the feast. "Not so many families have animals now," a young Uzbeki says with a shrug of his shoulders. "So there may not be a kid or lamb for the Bairam feast. But there is sure to be a celebration with plenty of good food."

A Wedding Day in Central Asia

The teahouse, or *chai khana*, is set back from the busy road in a quiet grove of shade trees, but today it is a lively place. A family is bustling about, making preparations for a wedding celebration.

Young boys are sweeping the wooden platforms under the trees and the open veranda where many of the guests will sit cross-legged on quilted mats around low tables. Platforms, tables, and veranda are all painted the soft blue which is a favorite color in these Asian lands.

The men of the family are cooking the rice *pilaff* or *plov* at open hearths off to one side. The rice is flavored with garlic, raisins, or quince, and probably some carrots. When it is puffed and light, it will be heaped on huge shallow serving dishes.

Other men are turning the smoking spits on which meat is roasting. Chunks of mutton on skewers sizzle as they brown. And since this is a special occasion, there are also chickens and plump quail. The spicy fragrance of the food will bring the children running. With the meal everyone will drink green tea from round china bowls.

Meanwhile the bridal couple has gone to the wedding palace in the city for the marriage ceremony. With some family members and a few friends, the young couple enters a room where a government official, seated at a table, greets them. The civil ceremony takes a very few moments. It is mainly a matter of recording the names of the young couple. Then the bride and groom exchange rings, to be worn on the right hands. In another room of the wedding palace, glasses may have been arranged on tables for a toast to the newlyweds. That toast does not take long either.

Everyone is eager to get on to the real celebration. Families with large enough homes, or big courtyards, like to have their celebrations at home. But most families in the Soviet Union live in small apartments, so their big parties, like this one, are held in restaurants.

In Uzbekistan, Tajikstan, and other central Asian republics, the place to go for a celebration is a teahouse. There are many of them, set in shady parks beside shallow pools, or on riverbanks. In a good big chai khana it is possible to follow the friendly

old central Asian custom of inviting everyone around to join in the feasting and fun.

First comes the feasting. When everyone has eaten his fill, some of the men may entertain the group with a battle of wits. This game is called *payr*. One makes a joking remark about the other. The second quickly replies with a witty retort. Back and forth the jokes fly, until one of the rivals cannot reply quickly enough to suit the crowd. Then the other is proclaimed the winner.

Next some of the young people appear. Wearing masks, they present a little playlet that makes gentle fun of the faults all people have. There is hearty laughter as the audience recognizes the boastful young show-off or the shy, clumsy young farmer at a far table as the subject of the fun.

By this time the musicians are tuning up. Soon the air vibrates with rhythmic sound. The lively tunes set the men to dancing, chests out, elbows cocked, heels clicking.

An automobile stands at the door, hung with streamers and with small dolls decorating the hood. It is waiting for the bridal couple. But the music and dancing are so lively that the car may have a long wait. This wedding party seems likely to go on all night.

A Baltic Holiday of Song—Early August

The road runs close to the seashore at the outskirts of the centuries-old Baltic seaport city of Tallin. Along it the last late-comers hurry toward an open-air amphitheater. They enter the amphitheater high on the hillslope. Below them on all sides stretch benches filled with attentive people.

At the foot of the hill lies a very wide stage. It is crowded with more than 2,000 men and women standing in close rows. These are only part of the singers gathered for the song festival known as *Ligo*. Choirs and choruses have come from many miles around. As many as 30,000 men and women will sing in the festival before it ends.

There is at least one singing society in every community of Estonia, of which Tallin is the capital. Neighboring Latvia and Lithuania have many too. Each of the three republics has a song festival of its own, in which every singing society takes part.

All year these societies meet to practice their four-part harmony. During the long, cold winters in the lands along the Baltic, people feel a need to gather in groups for indoor activities. Singing is a favorite one.

On Sundays the members sing in church. Churches in the Baltic countries—mostly Protestant—are often crowded for Sunday services. And for many people, the most important part of the service is the singing. The very walls of the buildings quiver as waves of lovely sound rise from hundreds of throats.

The choruses also entertain at special events in their towns throughout the year. But the high point for them all is the summer festival of song.

The celebration is not really limited to singing. Exhibitions of painting and craft work, performances by orchestras and dance troops, and readings of poetry also have a place in the summer festival. But the climax for which everyone waits is the time when all the choirs and choruses march through the streets of the city. Dressed in beautiful old embroidered blouses, bright skirts and crisp aprons or in snug knickers, bright sleeveless vests and white shirts under flat-brimmed hats, the singers make a fine spectacle indeed. Townsfolk line the streets to watch them pass.

And when those choirs march onto the stage and begin to sing, even the rustling trees on the hills around seem to still their leaves to revel in the floods of beautiful sound.

National Sports Day

Outside the huge sports arena—every Soviet city has one—banners flutter from a long row of flag-poles. From inside come the swelling shouts of the crowd gathered for National Sports Day. It does not matter much what the sport is at the moment— soccer, volleyball, or track. Russians are enthusiastic about them all.

They start at an early age competing in their schools and in Young Pioneers Camps. The best players from a school enter city competitions. Each city sends its best to district tournaments. The winners at the district meet go on to the finals for their republic. Finally at the All–Soviet Union games, the champions are chosen.

Some areas, of course, have purely regional sports. It would be hard, for example, to find anyone in the southernmost republic of Armenia to compete with the Yakut champion at reindeer racing. But for most sports Soviet training is almost as standardized as schoolroom studies. Track stars from the mountains of central Asia may find themselves competing with rivals from the marsh country of Byelorussia far to the west, or with others from mining towns north of the Arctic Circle. Wherever they are, whatever their sport, there is sure to be an eager crowd to cheer for a good performance.

4. THE HARVEST IS IN

Wheat Harvest in Russia

On an open stretch of ground near the collective farm buildings, long tables have been set up under the white-barked birch trees. Lanterns swing from low branches, and an orchestra seated on a small platform nearby strums and blares out lively tunes.

A few men and women still sit around the table, visiting. But the feast is over. Only a few crumbs remain on plates that were heaped high with bread, dark brown and white. A few limp slices of cucumber, some bits of parsley, onion, and other greens lie on platters. A few spoonfuls of thick cabbage and meat soup remain in the big soup pot. One small meat pie here has been overlooked, a pickled mushroom or two there. A forest of empty bottles rises above the dishes on the nearly deserted table.

Most of the feasters have been pulled from the table by the lively beat of the music. They are dancing, red-faced and bright-eyed. These are farm workers. They have brought in their harvest, and it was a good one. They have earned this night of fun.

Cotton Harvest in Uzbekistan

Cotton is king in Uzbekistan and in part of neighboring Khazakistan as well. When the fluffy bolls of "white gold," ready for processing, have been heaped into mounds as high as a two-story building, it is time to celebrate the harvest.

In cities like Bukhara, a harvest of cotton still seems a little strange to some of the old folks. They remember the years before all the long irrigation canals were cut across the deserts. Then most Uzbeki families wandered with their flocks from one parched pasture to the next. They carried with them, on horses or camels, the curved poles and the rolled coverings of their round portable homes.

80

Now most people live in modern apartments, or in settled town homes built of sun-dried brick, neatly whitewashed. Irrigation water to make crops grow has brought about great changes in their lives.

At the time of the cotton harvest, streets in Bukhara and other towns are lively. Of course there is always a parade as part of the festivity. Government officials make speeches praising the good work of the collective farmers and the size of the crop. Programs with singing and dancing are given in the workers' clubs too.

For young people, though, the dancing in the open squares of the city is the most fun. The high, coaxing strains of dance music drift down every lane, drawing out the young folk. In the old days, Uzbeki women were seldom seen in public places. But today in the Soviet society girls have as lively a time as boys at the cotton harvest festival.

Grape Harvest in the Caucasus

It is mid-September in the Caucasus. The hot summer sun shining down on mountain slopes of Armenia and Georgia—and on the hills of Moldavia

too—has done its work well. In every vineyard the vines are heavy with grapes in great, drooping bunches, ready to be harvested.

Buses leaving the cities are crowded these days. Everyone has relatives in some mountain village, and the time of the grape festival seems the best season to visit them.

Soon, in the towns and villages along the curving mountain roads, balconies and walls of homes are hung with garlands of grape leaves. Carts and trucks rumble along the roads, heaped high with grapes. Teams of young people picnic at the roadsides, resting after their hours of picking.

A few baskets of grapes go home to be made into sweets. The women boil down the rich purple juice, adding nuts—usually walnuts—as the juice thickens. Then it is poured out in a thin layer to dry in the sun. When the sheet is rolled up and cut into pieces, it is known as *churchkhela*, a favorite chewy candy.

Most of the grapes are squeezed through a press, so the sweet, frothy juice can be made into wine. Each village has its own special wine, and of course it must be sampled as soon as it is ready.

People gather at some open spot in the town, shaded by fine old trees. There they sip the new wine and eat *shashlyk*, chunks of spicy mutton roasted on a spit over an open fire. The men offer toasts as they lift their glasses. Everyone joins in the singing of hearty folk songs, and the young people dance under the trees. Dancing and singing go on around the clock at grape harvest time.

In the old days barefoot harvesters used to stamp the grapes in great vats. When the juice had been collected, the skins were thrown out in the farmyards. Cows, chickens, and geese would gather to lick, peck, or gobble up the spicy-sweet skins. They would eat until they wobbled as they walked.

Wine-making has been modernized in recent years, but the grape harvest is still celebrated with singing and dancing and feasting, much as it was years ago.

Mushroom Harvest in Byelorussia

Workers on their way home stop to read a notice on the factory bulletin board. A bus will be at the factory gate the following Saturday morning, the notice says. It will take workers and their families out to the woods for a morning of mushrooming. On Saturday morning, family groups begin to gather near the factory gate almost before daylight. They have packets of lunch in their sweater pockets and empty baskets over their arms.

It is not a very long drive out of town on a good highway to the woods. There the families soon scatter down grassy paths under the tall trees. Most people wear high boots, because the tall grasses and bushes are wet with dew. Also, the lowlands are likely to be marshy, with bogs into which one may sink halfway to the knees.

It takes a light touch to break off the spongy mushrooms at the ground without squeezing them, but even the small children out on their first hunt soon get the feel of the picking. They are very careful not to pick a poisonous variety.

Mushrooms are delicious quickly cooked in a little butter, but the big basketfuls a family brings home are far too many to eat all at once. Those that are left over are pickled in brine in big earthenware crocks. They are a reminder of harvest-time fun that can be enjoyed all winter.

5. WHEN WINTER COMES

The Anniversary of the Revolution—November 7–8

Jet planes thunder over the Kremlin and Red Square in close formation. Their white vapor trails stand out sharply against the low gray winter sky.

The snow has been cleared from the pavement of Moscow's Red Square. But paving stones still gleam wetly as heavy military tanks in stately columns rumble by, followed by wide-wheeled trucks carrying huge guns.

The officials viewing this impressive parade from their places of honor on top of Lenin's tomb are wearing heavy overcoats, caps, and gloves against the cold. For November 7 is well into winter in

Moscow. The crowds of people lined up behind the barricades that edge the square are wrapped in their warmest winter clothes. Even the colored lights strung along the streets look cold by day.

It was a dark, cold day in 1917, too, when the Bolsheviks stormed the Winter Palace in Petrograd (now Leningrad). That action began the revolution that put the Communists in control of the government. Now every year on the anniversary of the beginning of that revolution, the Communists proudly display the power of their government in a huge parade of military might.

The uprising is known as the "October Revolution" because it started on October 25 according to the old Russian calendar. When the Soviet government switched to the western calendar to be in accord with most of the rest of the world, this date became November 7. This is why the "October Revolution" is now celebrated on November 7.

It was an armed uprising, so it is natural that it should be celebrated with a military parade. Until a few years ago, the May Day parade also was a military parade. All the newest and most powerful weapons and vehicles of the Soviet armed forces appeared then. Sometimes they were shown to the world for the first time during the parade.

In recent years, the leaders of the government decided that only one day a year will be devoted to big military parades. May Day was turned over to workers and students. Now the most important military celebrations are on November 7. All over the vast Soviet Union, even to the farthest reaches of arctic Siberia, these parades are held; huge banners are hung; and everywhere people celebrate.

The Soviet Union is proud of the men in its armed services. Each of the services has its own holiday. Navy Day, for example, features the Soviet fleet on display in the harbors of Leningrad on the Baltic, Odessa on the Black Sea, and Vladivostok on the Pacific. Army Day in February and Aviation Day in August have their own parades, air shows, and fireworks. On November 7, though, soldiers, sailors, and airmen all march.

Troops representing the widespread areas of the Soviet Union join forces in the display. Some of the most dashing are cavalry units from central Asia.

The riders rein in their gleaming mounts as they pass the reviewing stand. All the men salute the officials smartly, but with true military discipline not an eye flickers in that direction. All Soviet military men are at their very best on the seventh of November, their own great holiday.

Christmas

"Does anyone still celebrate Christmas?" a visitor asked a young Armenian not long ago.

"But of course," he replied with a shrug of the shoulders.

The response was similar in neighboring Georgia. And it is true in the Baltic republics far to the north of the Caucasus Mountains. Christmas is still kept, even though it is not quite the same as thirty years ago.

Then on Christmas Eve every home in the Baltic republics was fragrant with the spicy smell of a fresh-cut Christmas tree. Ornaments of thin colored glass or of pale golden straw were tucked among the green needles. For light, small twisted candles in metal holders were clipped to the branches.

Late on Christmas Eve everyone went to church. Perhaps as a special treat, a horse-drawn sleigh was hired for the occasion. Dressed in warm coats, caps, and mittens, the family piled into the sleigh and tucked thick lap robes around feet and knees.

At the crack of the driver's whip, the horses started off. Sleigh bells tinkled as the runners slid smoothly over the snow through the crisp and starry night. Ahead lay the brightly lighted church with its own gaily decorated Christmas tree, this one perhaps twenty feet tall.

If the children were a bit restless during the service, it was because they were eager to be home again. There a table set with food was waiting for them. And before the midnight supper was finished, a knock sounded at the door.

The children knew what that meant! Someone hurried to open the door, and in walked the Old Man of Christmas himself, wearing a knitted cap and long coat. Best of all, over his shoulder swung a bulging bag that held toys for all the young people. Everyone had something new to show when the family went to visit the grandparents on Christmas Day.

In villages of Russia and the Ukraine, boys and girls went from house to house singing carols on Christmas Eve. Only the older folks were left at home to welcome the carolers, but they opened the door to every group. And in came the boys and girls, laughing and joking, their cheeks and noses glowing from the cold.

Sometimes a group made their calls in costumes representing the Three Kings or Wise Men who came from distant lands to visit the Christ Child when he was born in Bethlehem. When they came into a home, they presented a little playlet.

Each boy and girl carried a sack. Everywhere they stopped, they were given something for their sacks— fruit and nuts and curd dumplings for the most part. Sometimes the gift was sausage or bread in small white loaves. There might even be a copper coin or two.

Some of these old customs have died away or changed their form. But groups of young people still like to give little plays. They still like to frolic in the snow. They still receive small gifts at holiday time, though it may be that Father Frost brings them now in place of the Old Man of Christmas. Tall pine trees, aglitter with ornaments and lights, still delight the eye and heart. And actually Christmas itself is still quietly celebrated in many homes in the Soviet Union, even though officially New Year's celebrations have taken its place.

As for New Year's Day, that is where this book began.

PRONOUNCING GUIDE

The accented syllable in each word is written in capital letters.

Azerbaidzhan	ah zur bye JUN
Bairam	BAY rom *or* Bay ROM
blini	blee NEE
Buryats	boor YATS
chai khana	CHY khah NAH
djigits	ju GEETS
icon	EYE con (in English)
	ee KON (in Russian)
Kazan	kah ZAN
Kirghiz	ker GEEZ
Komsomol	kom soh MOL
Kop Karim	kop kah REEM
kulich	koo LEECH
kumiss	koo MISS
Kuz kumai	KUZ ku my
Ligo	LEE go
Novosibirsk	NO vo si BIRSK
Oktobriades	ok TOE bree OD ees (in English)
	ok to bri AT tsi (in Russian)
pashka	PAS kha
payr	PAY r
pilaff	pea LOFF
pirok	pi ROAK *or* pi ROAG
Saban Tuy	sa BAN too ey
Subbotnik	soob BOTE nik
Tajik	tah JIK
Tatar	tah TAR
troika	TROI ka
Uzbek	OOZ bek
Ysyakh	ee SIK

INDEX